ASOGWA JUSTINA

Mind Ventures: Pushing the Boundaries of Thought

Contents

1

The Mysterious Benefactor

Dr. Ethan Harper's lab was a sanctuary of organized chaos. Shelves lined with tomes on quantum mechanics and neuroscience stood in stark contrast to the scattered notes and half-empty coffee mugs cluttering the work surfaces. A single overhead light illuminated the whiteboard, covered with complex equations and sketches that seemed to pulsate with an unspoken promise of brilliance.

It was late in the evening when the heavy wooden door creaked open, causing Ethan to glance up from his latest experiment. He was alone, or so he thought. The usual hum of the lab equipment and the soft ticking of the wall clock were interrupted by the faint sound of footsteps, muffled by the thick carpet.

"Who's there?" Ethan called, his voice echoing through the empty lab. There was no reply, only the eerie silence of the building's late-night calm.

He shook his head and returned to his work, attributing the noise to his imagination. It wasn't uncommon for his mind to play tricks on him after hours of intense focus. The project he was working on was ambitious—a theoretical framework for harnessing cognitive potential that could redefine the boundaries of human thought. But the isolation, the constant pressure to make a breakthrough, was beginning to take its toll.

Just as he adjusted a complex circuit on his workstation, a sharp knock on the door startled him. Ethan hesitated, then walked over and opened it, but there was no one in the corridor. Only a small, unmarked envelope lay on the floor.

He picked it up and examined it. The envelope was plain, devoid of any identifying marks, but its weight was substantial. With a mixture of curiosity and apprehension, he tore it open. Inside was a single sheet of paper, typewritten, and neatly folded. Ethan unfolded it, revealing a message:

Dr. Harper,

Your work is impressive, but it lacks the final element that could elevate it to revolutionary status. I am prepared to offer you the resources you need to complete your project. All I require is that you finish it within thirty days.

Contact me at the address below if you accept this offer.

—A Friend

Below the message was an address—one he didn't recognize. There was no name, no further explanation. The letter was unsigned, its anonymity adding to the unsettling nature of the note.

Ethan's mind raced. Who could this "Friend" be? Why would someone offer him such a substantial help without revealing their identity? His heart pounded with both excitement and trepidation. This could be the opportunity he had been waiting for, the missing piece to his research. But the secrecy, the lack of any clear motive, unnerved him.

He scanned the letter again, trying to discern any hidden meanings or clues. The clean typewritten font was devoid of any personal touch, and the lack of a return address offered no leads. It was as if the sender was deliberately shrouding themselves in mystery.

Despite the unease, Ethan felt a surge of hope. He had been working on his project for years, and while his theories were groundbreaking, he had struggled with securing the necessary resources for practical application. This offer could be the breakthrough he desperately needed. But what were the terms of this mysterious agreement? And why the urgency of thirty days?

He decided to investigate the address mentioned in the letter. Pulling up a map on his computer, he traced the location. It was in a secluded part of the city, an old warehouse district that had been largely abandoned. The area was known for its derelict buildings and a general air of neglect. It was an odd choice for a meeting place, especially given the importance of the offer.

Ethan's thoughts were interrupted by a sudden jolt—his computer screen flickered, then went dark. The lab's lights dimmed briefly before returning to normal. He frowned, checking the power connections and rebooting his machine. As he did, he glanced around the lab, feeling an inexplicable chill.

Just then, his phone buzzed with an incoming message. It was from an unknown number. Hesitant, he opened the text. The message contained a single line: "Trust no one. Meet me at the address." The sender's anonymity added another layer of mystery and danger.

He felt a shiver down his spine. The message was chillingly similar in tone to the letter. Was this another part of the elaborate game, or was it a warning? His instincts told him to be cautious, but the potential for a breakthrough was too tempting.

Determined to uncover the truth, Ethan resolved to visit the address the following evening. He knew he had to be cautious. If this was a trap, he needed to be prepared. He began to gather his belongings, securing his notes and sensitive data, ensuring nothing would be compromised if he was followed or if something went awry.

As he locked the lab and stepped into the cool night air, the weight of the decision settled on him. He could feel the gravity of the situation, the sense of something looming just out of sight. The possibility of a major advancement in his research was tantalizing, but the shrouded threats and veiled intentions were unsettling.

With a mix of anticipation and dread, Ethan set off towards the address, knowing that the next few days could change everything. The lab behind him seemed to exhale a sigh of relief as he left, as if sensing the beginning of a new, uncertain chapter in his life.

2

The Disappearing Genius

The warehouse district was a maze of shadowed alleys and derelict structures. The streets, once bustling with activity, now lay in eerie silence, illuminated only by the occasional flicker of a distant streetlamp. The address from the letter led Ethan to an old, dilapidated building at the edge of the district, its brick facade covered in grime and neglect. The large metal doors were rusted, and the windows were shattered or boarded up.

Ethan's footsteps echoed off the cracked pavement as he approached the entrance. His breath came in steady puffs, visible in the chill of the night air. He glanced at his watch; the meeting was set for midnight. He had arrived early, hoping to scout the area and assess any potential risks before the rendezvous.

The building appeared abandoned, its darkened windows revealing nothing but shadows. Ethan reached the heavy metal door and noticed an old-fashioned keyhole beneath a faded sign reading, "Authorized Personnel Only." He hesitated, then reached into his pocket for the letter. The address matched the one on the letter, but he had not received any further instructions. This uncertainty made him uneasy.

The sound of distant footsteps made Ethan stiffen. He pressed his back against the cold wall, straining to listen. The footsteps grew louder, approaching from the street behind him. His mind raced with possibilities—was someone following him, or was it merely the sound of the district's decay?

Peering around the corner, Ethan saw a figure moving cautiously toward the warehouse. The figure was clad in a dark coat, their face obscured by a hat pulled low. The mysterious figure paused before the entrance, fumbling with something in their hands. Ethan could barely make out the outline of a key being inserted into the lock.

Ethan's heart pounded as he realized the figure was likely the contact mentioned in the letter. They seemed to struggle with the lock, their movements agitated. After a few moments, the door creaked open, and the figure slipped inside. Ethan took a deep breath, weighing his options. He could retreat, but his curiosity and the promise of crucial resources compelled him to follow.

He waited until the door had closed behind the figure, then moved quietly to the entrance. The door was slightly ajar, just enough for him to slip through. Ethan eased it open and entered the darkened interior.

The warehouse was a cavernous space, filled with the smell of mildew and old wood. Dust motes floated in the sparse beams of moonlight that filtered through the broken windows. The sound of Ethan's footsteps was swallowed by the oppressive silence. He scanned the area, noting the scattered debris and the few scattered crates and barrels.

Ahead, a faint light flickered from an open doorway at the far end of the warehouse. Ethan approached cautiously, his senses on high alert. The light grew brighter as he neared, revealing a narrow corridor leading to another room. The air felt heavy with anticipation as he followed the light.

Reaching the doorway, Ethan peered inside. The room was a stark contrast to the dilapidated warehouse—a well-organized space filled with cutting-edge technology and research equipment. It was as if he had stepped into a high-tech lab, far removed from the surrounding decay. His eyes were drawn to the figure at the center of the room.

The figure, now visible in the light, was not the person Ethan had expected. Instead of a mysterious benefactor, he saw Dr. Marcus Hale, a renowned scientist known for his pioneering work in cognitive enhancement. Hale was hunched over a workbench, absorbed in a complex array of electronic devices and papers.

Ethan's surprise was quickly replaced by concern. Hale was supposed to be missing, his sudden disappearance a major topic in the scientific community. The thought of finding Hale here, working on something, raised more questions than answers. Was this somehow connected to the mysterious letter?

As Ethan stepped into the room, his presence triggered an alert on one of the monitors. Hale looked up, his face showing a mixture of shock and recognition.

"Ethan Harper," Hale said, his voice taut with a mixture of relief and anxiety. "What are you doing here?"

"I received a letter," Ethan replied, trying to sound calm. "It led me to this address. I didn't expect to find you here."

Hale's expression shifted to one of guarded apprehension. "The letter was meant for me. I've been working on something critical, and I've had to stay hidden. The situation is more complex than you know."

Before Ethan could respond, the sound of the warehouse door slamming shut echoed through the corridor. Both men turned in alarm. Hale's face went pale as he quickly moved to secure the room. He activated a locking mechanism on the door and began hastily gathering his papers and equipment.

"What's going on?" Ethan demanded.

Hale looked grim. "Someone knows we're here. They've found us."

Ethan's heart raced as he glanced around, searching for any sign of intrusion. The warehouse's eerie silence was punctuated by the faint sound of footsteps and muffled voices from outside the room. Hale's anxiety was palpable as he continued to pack away sensitive materials.

The dim light from the monitors cast flickering shadows on the walls, making the room feel even more claustrophobic. Ethan could sense the urgency in Hale's movements and felt a growing sense of dread.

"Who could have found us?" Ethan asked.

Hale shook his head. "I don't know, but it's not safe here. We need to leave before they breach the room."

Just as Hale finished securing the last of his equipment, the door rattled violently. Someone was trying to force their way in. Hale grabbed a briefcase and motioned for Ethan to follow. They quickly exited through a side door, leading them into a network of hidden tunnels beneath the warehouse.

As they moved through the dimly lit tunnels, Ethan's mind raced with questions. What had led Hale to this hidden lab? Why had he disappeared, and what was the nature of the work that had caused such danger?

The tunnels were cold and damp, with the sound of dripping water creating an unsettling atmosphere. Hale led the way with a flashlight, his pace quick and determined. Ethan struggled to keep up, the weight of the situation settling heavily on his shoulders.

Finally, Hale stopped at a small, inconspicuous door. He unlocked it and ushered Ethan inside. The room beyond was a modest, yet well-equipped safe house. Hale quickly set up his equipment and began assessing the situation.

Ethan watched, his mind swirling with the implications. The disappearance of Dr. Hale, the mysterious letter, and now the potential threat looming over them. The stakes were higher than he had anticipated, and the journey into the unknown had only just begun.

3

The Unseen Rival

The safe house, though modest, was a stark contrast to the chaos Ethan had left behind in the warehouse. It was meticulously organized, with clean, functional furnishings and walls lined with technical diagrams and maps. The air was filled with the faint hum of electronics and the occasional clink of metal as Dr. Marcus Hale worked to reassemble his equipment.

Ethan watched in silence as Hale methodically connected cables and booted up a series of monitors. The room's only window was covered with heavy blinds, casting the space in a dim, artificial glow. Ethan could sense the tension in Hale's movements; the urgency was palpable.

Hale glanced up, his face drawn and weary. "We're safe here for now, but I need to know exactly why you're here, Ethan."

Ethan hesitated, weighing his words. "I received a letter directing me to the warehouse. It mentioned someone could help me with my project. When I arrived, I found you instead."

Hale's eyes narrowed, a mix of frustration and curiosity flickering across his face. "The letter was supposed to be a signal, a way to get my attention. But if you received it, then someone else must be involved. Someone who wants to make sure we don't succeed."

Ethan felt a chill run down his spine. "Who could want to sabotage our work? And why?"

Hale paused, clearly grappling with how much to reveal. "I've been working on something highly sensitive—an advanced cognitive enhancement system that could revolutionize the field. But the technology is powerful and potentially dangerous. There are factions out there that don't want such advancements to see the light of day."

Ethan's mind raced. "And you think this is why they were trying to get to you tonight?"

"Yes," Hale said. "It's more than just a personal threat. There are powerful interests at stake. If my research falls into the wrong hands, it could be catastrophic."

The room fell into a heavy silence, punctuated only by the faint clicking of Hale's keyboard as he typed rapidly. Ethan's thoughts churned with the implications of Hale's revelations. If what Hale was working on was as significant as he claimed, the stakes had just become much higher.

Hale finally looked up from his work. "We need to figure out who's behind this and how they knew about the warehouse. There's a chance they might have been monitoring our communications."

Ethan's thoughts flashed back to the letter, the cryptic message, and the sudden appearance of the unknown rival. He wondered if the same forces that had targeted Hale might also be aware of his own research. "What should we do next?"

Hale moved to a locked cabinet and retrieved a set of files and a portable drive. "We need to secure the data and find out who is tracking us. I have contacts who can help, but first, we need to lay low and assess the situation."

As Hale began transferring sensitive data to the portable drive, Ethan's attention was drawn to a sudden noise—a sharp knock at the door. Both men froze, their eyes meeting in alarm. Hale quickly disconnected the drive and stuffed it into a hidden compartment beneath a loose floorboard.

"Stay quiet," Hale whispered. "I'll check who it is."

Hale moved stealthily to the door and peered through the peephole. His face went pale, and he turned back to Ethan with a look of grim determination. "It's someone from the outside. They're checking the building."

Ethan's heart raced. The knock came again, more insistent this time. Hale motioned for Ethan to stay low and quickly went to a corner of the room where he pulled out a small surveillance camera. He connected it to the monitors and viewed the footage from the door.

On the screen, a shadowy figure in a dark suit was examining the door and the surrounding area with a professional air. They carried an air of authority and confidence that suggested they were no ordinary investigator.

"They're not here by accident," Hale muttered, eyes fixed on the screen. "They're searching for something or someone. We need to be careful."

Ethan nodded, his mind racing. The appearance of such a skilled individual raised the stakes. Whoever was behind this had resources and knew how to use them. The situation was more dangerous than he had initially realized.

Hale moved back to the workbench and began rifling through a drawer, pulling out various tools and gadgets. "We need to create a diversion and get out of here. I have an old escape route, but it's risky. It'll take us through the sewers, but it's our best chance."

Ethan felt a surge of anxiety. "The sewers? Are you sure it's safe?"

"It's the only option we have," Hale said firmly. "We'll have to move quickly. I'll set up a false lead to throw them off our trail."

Hale worked swiftly, preparing a series of documents and placing them in a folder marked with misleading information. He set the folder on a table near the door, making it look as though it had been left in haste. He then set a small device to trigger an alarm, ensuring that the investigators would be led away by the commotion.

As the device beeped and the alarm echoed through the building, Hale gestured for Ethan to follow. They moved silently through the back corridors of the safe house, slipping through a hidden door and into the cramped, dark tunnel system beneath the building.

The smell of damp earth and decay filled the air as they navigated the narrow, winding tunnels. Ethan's flashlight illuminated the walls, revealing the grime and neglect of the underground passage. The sound of dripping water and distant echoes added to the oppressive atmosphere.

Hale led the way with a practiced ease, his movements deliberate and purposeful. Ethan followed closely, his thoughts racing with the gravity of their situation. The rival's presence, the mysterious threats, and the urgency of their escape weighed heavily on him.

As they emerged from the tunnels into the night, Ethan looked back at the now distant safe house. The sense of urgency had only intensified. The rival's search, Hale's warnings, and the unknown threats all converged into a dangerous web of intrigue and danger. The journey ahead promised to be fraught with uncertainty, and Ethan knew they needed to act quickly to uncover the truth and protect their work.

With a final glance at the darkened safe house, Ethan and Hale moved into the night, determined to navigate the treacherous landscape of espionage and deceit that lay ahead.

4

The Shadows of Betrayal

The night air was cold and biting as Ethan and Dr. Marcus Hale emerged from the sewer system into the secluded alley. The distant hum of the city seemed eerily quiet in the early hours before dawn. Hale led the way with a flashlight, their only source of illumination in the inky darkness. Ethan's mind raced as they navigated through the maze of narrow streets and abandoned buildings.

Hale's earlier assurances that they would be safe for now provided little comfort. The tension was palpable, hanging between them like a thick fog. Ethan's thoughts swirled with questions: Who was the shadowy figure at the warehouse? Why were they so intent on disrupting Hale's research? And, most importantly, who could he trust?

As they rounded a corner, Hale stopped abruptly and held up a hand. He motioned for Ethan to be silent and listened intently. The distant echo of footsteps could be heard, gradually growing louder. Hale's face tightened with concern.

"We're not alone," Hale whispered. "Someone's closing in on us."

Ethan's heart pounded in his chest. The chase through the tunnels had left him on edge, and the thought of being pursued only heightened his anxiety. Hale's flashlight flickered briefly, casting unsettling shadows on the walls around them.

They took cover behind a stack of old crates, trying to blend into the darkness. Hale's breathing was steady, but Ethan could see the strain in his eyes. The footsteps grew closer, and Hale pulled out a small device from his coat pocket. It emitted a faint, pulsing light—a tracking beacon that Hale had used to mislead their pursuers.

"Let's move," Hale instructed. "We need to get to a safe location where we can regroup."

They slipped through the alleyways with practiced stealth, Hale guiding them through the labyrinthine network of streets. The city's deserted warehouses and darkened storefronts provided ample cover, but the sense of imminent danger made every creak and rustle seem magnified.

After what felt like an eternity of winding through darkened streets, Hale finally stopped at an old, unmarked door set into the side of a brick building. The door was rusted and appeared to be part of an old storage unit. Hale produced a set of keys and unlocked it with a practiced ease.

Inside, the room was surprisingly well-kept—a stark contrast to the grime of the surrounding area. The small space was filled with maps, documents, and various pieces of equipment. Hale quickly went to work, pulling out a large map and spreading it on a table.

"This is where we'll be for the next few hours," Hale said, his voice steady but his eyes betraying a hint of exhaustion. "We need to figure out who's after us and what they want."

Ethan glanced around the room, taking in the organized chaos of Hale's setup. The walls were covered with notes and photographs, some pinned with red string connecting various points. Hale's research was evidently extensive and meticulously detailed.

"I don't understand," Ethan said, trying to process the gravity of the situation. "Who would want to sabotage your work so badly? What's at stake?"

Hale took a deep breath, clearly grappling with how much to reveal. "My research involves cognitive enhancement—potentially unlocking abilities beyond our current understanding. It's groundbreaking, but it also poses significant risks. Some factions view it as a threat to their interests or as a weapon that could shift the balance of power."

Ethan's eyes widened as he absorbed Hale's explanation. The implications of such technology were staggering, and the potential for abuse was immense. "So, who do you think is behind this?"

Before Hale could answer, there was a sudden noise—a soft tapping at the door. Both men tensed, exchanging worried glances. Hale moved cautiously to the door, peeking through a small window. His face turned ashen.

"It's someone we know," Hale said, his voice low. "A former colleague of mine, a researcher named Julia Cline. She was once part of my team but left under strained circumstances."

Ethan felt a knot form in his stomach. Julia Cline was a name he recognized—an accomplished scientist with a reputation for both brilliance and controversy. If she was involved, it added a troubling layer of complexity to their predicament.

Hale opened the door cautiously, and a woman stepped inside. Julia Cline's expression was a mix of concern and resolve. She was dressed in practical, professional attire, her eyes scanning the room with a sharp, calculating gaze.

"Marcus," she said, her voice steady. "I didn't expect to find you here. We need to talk."

Ethan watched as Hale's demeanor shifted from apprehensive to guarded. "Julia, what are you doing here? How did you find us?"

Cline's gaze flicked to Ethan, assessing him with a mix of curiosity and suspicion. "I have my ways. And I'm here because I've been following the developments in your research. When I heard about the threats, I knew I had to act."

Hale's expression was one of strained patience. "And what do you want from us, Julia?"

Cline stepped further into the room, her posture firm. "I want to help, but we need to be honest with each other. The stakes are too high for any more secrets."

Ethan felt the tension in the room thicken. The dynamics between Hale and Cline were fraught with unspoken history and unresolved conflict. He could sense that their past relationship was a crucial piece of the puzzle.

Cline pulled out a folder from her bag and handed it to Hale. "I've been working with a contact who has information about the group pursuing you. They've been tracking your work for months. They have their own agenda, and it's not one that we can ignore."

Hale took the folder, his eyes scanning the documents inside. His expression shifted from surprise to grim realization. "This is worse than I thought. If they're targeting us with this level of precision, they're preparing for something major."

Ethan looked between Hale and Cline, trying to grasp the full scope of the situation. "What can we do to counter this? How do we stay ahead of them?"

Cline took a deep breath. "We need to understand their motives and their next moves. I've arranged for a secure meeting with one of my contacts who has insights into their operations. It's risky, but it might give us the information we need to anticipate their actions."

Hale nodded, his resolve hardening. "Alright. Let's set up a plan. We need to stay ahead of them and ensure that our work doesn't fall into the wrong hands."

As the first light of dawn began to filter through the small window of the room, the three of them set to work. The sense of urgency and danger was palpable. The shadows of betrayal loomed large, and the path forward was fraught with uncertainty. They were on a precipice, and every decision they made could tip the balance between success and disaster.

With Cline's unexpected arrival and the new information she brought, the stakes had risen significantly. Ethan and Hale were now facing an even greater challenge, and the true extent of the threat against them was just beginning to unfold.

5

Echoes in the Dark

The sky was still shrouded in the inky black of pre-dawn when Ethan, Dr. Marcus Hale, and Julia Cline emerged from the safe house, their senses heightened and nerves on edge. The city was eerily quiet, its usual hum of activity muted under the weight of anticipation and dread. The trio moved with a practiced stealth, blending into the shadows as they made their way through the winding streets towards their rendezvous point.

The meeting was set at an old, abandoned railway station on the outskirts of the city—an area that promised both isolation and security. Cline had arranged for them to meet a contact who purportedly had crucial information about their adversaries. The thought of potentially gaining insights into their pursuers was a small comfort amidst the growing tension.

Hale led the way, his flashlight cutting through the darkness. The old station loomed ahead, its once-grand entrance now a skeletal structure of rust and decay. Ethan's heart raced with a mixture of anxiety and anticipation. The feeling of being pursued was never far from his mind, and every shadow seemed to conceal a threat.

As they approached the entrance, Hale paused to survey the surroundings, his sharp eyes scanning for any sign of movement. "We need to be cautious," he whispered. "The station may be a trap, or it could be monitored."

Cline nodded, her expression serious. "We'll enter through the side door. It's less conspicuous, and we should avoid drawing attention."

They moved silently to a side entrance, Hale picking the lock with deft precision. The door creaked open, and they slipped inside, their footsteps echoing off the walls of the cavernous station. The interior was a desolate expanse, the remnants of old ticket counters and waiting areas shrouded in dust and cobwebs. The air was stale, and the silence was almost oppressive.

They made their way to a small office off to one side, where Cline's contact was supposed to meet them. Hale carefully pushed open the door, revealing a room cluttered with old maps, surveillance equipment, and scattered files. A single lamp illuminated the space with a dim, yellow light, casting long shadows that seemed to dance on the walls.

Sitting at a desk was a man in his early forties, dressed in a rumpled suit. His face was lined with age and stress, and he looked up with wary eyes as the trio entered. His name was Samuel Drake, a former intelligence officer with connections to various underground networks.

"Drake," Cline said, her voice steady but laced with urgency. "Thanks for coming."

Drake stood, his gaze flicking between Hale, Cline, and Ethan. "I didn't think you'd get here so soon. The word is that you've got some dangerous enemies on your tail."

Hale nodded. "We need to know who's behind this and what their next move might be."

Drake sighed and motioned for them to sit. "Alright. Let me brief you on what I've found. The group after you is known as the Black Veil. They're an elusive network with a reputation for being highly secretive and ruthless."

Ethan's stomach churned at the name. The Black Veil was notorious for its clandestine operations and ruthless tactics. "What do they want?"

Drake leaned forward, his voice dropping to a whisper. "They're interested in your work, Hale. They've been tracking your research for months. They believe that your cognitive enhancement system could give them a significant edge—either as a tool for manipulation or as a weapon."

Cline's eyes narrowed. "How do they know so much about us? And why are they targeting us now?"

Drake shuffled through some documents and handed a file to Hale. "They've been monitoring your communications and movements. As for why now—there's been a recent shift in their operations. They're preparing for something big, and they see your research as a key component."

Hale studied the file, his face growing darker with each passing moment. "What's their plan? How can we stop them?"

Drake glanced around nervously. "I don't have all the details, but I've intercepted some chatter that suggests they're planning a major operation. They might try to take you out before you can complete your work or even attempt to steal your research."

The gravity of the situation sank in, and Ethan felt a chill run down his spine. The Black Veil's plans were clearly far-reaching and dangerous. The possibility of having their work stolen or destroyed was a looming threat.

Suddenly, a loud crash echoed through the station, followed by shouts and the clatter of heavy boots. Panic flared in the room, and Ethan's heart raced. The sound of approaching footsteps grew louder, and it was clear that their time was running out.

Drake's face turned ashen. "They've found us. We need to get out of here, now!"

Hale quickly grabbed the file and stuffed it into a bag. "Follow me. There's a back exit we can use."

They dashed through the darkened corridors of the station, their footsteps pounding against the concrete. The noise of the approaching pursuers grew louder, their shouts echoing off the walls. The adrenaline surged through Ethan's veins as he pushed himself to keep pace with Hale and Cline.

Hale led them to a hidden passage behind a maintenance door. The passage was narrow and cramped, barely wide enough for them to move in single file. The sound of their pursuers grew fainter as they descended deeper into the passage.

As they emerged into a forgotten storage area, Hale stopped and took a deep breath. "We should be safe here for a moment, but we need to regroup and plan our next move."

Ethan leaned against the wall, catching his breath. "How did they find us so quickly?"

Drake, his face still pale, looked around nervously. "They must have been tracking us more closely than I realized. They're well-prepared and dangerous."

Cline glanced at Hale. "We need to move quickly and stay ahead of them. If they're closing in on us, they might be preparing for a larger assault."

Hale nodded, his expression resolute. "Agreed. We need to analyze the information Drake provided and devise a strategy to counter their plans. We can't afford to be caught off guard again."

With the immediate danger momentarily averted, the group took stock of their situation. The threat from the Black Veil was more imminent than ever, and their plans were growing increasingly complex. The stakes had never been higher, and Ethan knew that every decision they made from this point forward would be critical.

As the echoes of their pursuers faded into the distance, the shadows of betrayal and danger seemed to close in even tighter. The battle against the Black Veil had only just begun, and the path ahead was fraught with uncertainty and peril.

6

The Unseen Enemy

The first light of dawn crept through the cracked windows of the abandoned warehouse where Ethan, Hale, Cline, and Drake had taken refuge. The once-vibrant daylight seemed foreign now, casting harsh shadows across their weary faces. They had spent hours analyzing the documents Drake had provided, the gravity of their situation weighing heavily on them.

Hale stood by the window, peering out at the street below. His eyes were hard, reflecting the worry and exhaustion of the long night. Cline, seated at a makeshift desk, was poring over the maps and documents, her brow furrowed in concentration. Ethan, pacing nervously, could feel the tension in the room building.

Drake, visibly shaken, sat slumped in a corner. The adrenaline from their narrow escape had faded, leaving him visibly drained. "We need to get a handle on their next move," he said, his voice trembling. "We need to know what they're planning and how to stay ahead."

Hale turned from the window, his face set in determination. "We'll need to gather more intelligence. The Black Veil is elusive and dangerous. They're likely planning something big, and we need to anticipate their actions."

Cline nodded in agreement, her fingers tracing the routes on the map. "I've seen their tactics before. They're methodical and meticulous. If they're after Hale's research, they'll have a well-laid plan to obtain it."

The group fell silent, the enormity of the threat hanging in the air. Ethan glanced at the clock on the wall—time was slipping away. "What's our next move? We need to find a way to outmaneuver them."

As if on cue, the sound of distant sirens echoed through the warehouse. Ethan's heart skipped a beat. "We've been compromised," he said urgently. "They must have tracked us here."

Hale's face grew grim. "We need to move quickly. We can't afford to stay here any longer."

They gathered their belongings and slipped out of the warehouse, moving swiftly through the alleys and side streets. The city seemed to close in around them, the once-familiar streets now feeling alien and menacing. Hale led the way, his knowledge of the city's hidden routes guiding them through the labyrinthine network of urban decay.

After several hours of tense travel, they arrived at an inconspicuous safe house, one of Hale's well-placed hideouts. The place was secure and well-hidden, but the constant sense of danger made every creak and whisper feel amplified.

Inside, Hale quickly set up a temporary command center. He spread out the maps and documents they had recovered, studying them intently. "We need to find out where the Black Veil is operating from," he said, his voice steady despite the tension. "If we can locate their base of operations, we might be able to disrupt their plans."

Cline, her eyes tired but focused, began contacting her network of informants, hoping to gather any intel that might shed light on the Black Veil's activities. Drake, though exhausted, was still vigilant, keeping watch for any signs of pursuit.

Ethan's mind raced. The Black Veil's reach was extensive, and their methods were ruthless. He couldn't shake the feeling that they were always one step behind, constantly reacting to the moves of a formidable and unseen enemy.

As the hours ticked by, the room's tension grew palpable. Every sound, every sudden movement seemed to carry the weight of impending danger. Cline's phone rang, and she answered with a terse, urgent tone. "What do you have for me?"

Her expression changed from anxious to hopeful as she listened. "Are you sure? That's a lead we can follow. Thank you."

She hung up and turned to the group, her face reflecting a mixture of relief and anxiety. "I've got a lead on a possible location. It's a warehouse on the outskirts of the city. It's been flagged as a potential base for the Black Veil."

Hale nodded, his face set in determination. "That's a start. We need to check it out and see if we can gather more information."

They prepared to leave, each movement purposeful and focused. The sense of urgency was overwhelming, knowing that the Black Veil's plans might be coming to fruition.

As they made their way to the warehouse, the city's streets felt like a gauntlet of shadows and uncertainty. The familiar surroundings now seemed menacing, the fear of being watched or followed palpable. Hale led them with a sense of grim resolve, his knowledge of the city's hidden paths their only advantage.

The warehouse was located in a desolate area, surrounded by a chain-link fence and overgrown with weeds. The building itself was large and imposing, its exterior weathered and worn. Hale approached cautiously, his eyes scanning the area for any signs of activity.

They found a secluded vantage point from which to observe the warehouse. Through binoculars, they could see figures moving inside—cloaked in shadows and engaged in what looked like hurried preparations. The sight confirmed their worst fears: the Black Veil was indeed planning something significant.

Ethan's pulse quickened as he observed the scene. "What are they planning? And how do we stop them?"

Hale's expression was grim. "We need to get closer, gather as much information as we can, and find a way to counter their plans. But we must be careful. If they're aware of us, this could be a trap."

The group moved stealthily towards the warehouse, their every step calculated and cautious. The feeling of being hunted was inescapable, heightening every sound and shadow. They found a small, partially open door and slipped inside, their senses on high alert.

The interior of the warehouse was a maze of crates and machinery, the dim light casting eerie shadows across the floor. They moved quietly, their movements almost instinctive as they navigated through the cluttered space.

As they approached a central area, they could hear voices—low and tense—discussing plans and strategies. Ethan's heart pounded in his chest. They were close, so close to uncovering the Black Veil's plans.

Suddenly, a loud noise echoed through the warehouse—a clatter of metal and the sound of footsteps approaching. Panic surged through Ethan, and he exchanged worried glances with Hale and Cline.

Hale signaled for them to hide, and they quickly took cover behind a stack of crates. The footsteps grew louder, and the figures they had seen earlier emerged into view. The Black Veil operatives were dressed in tactical gear, their faces obscured by masks.

Ethan's breath caught in his throat as he watched them, his mind racing with the implications. They were on the brink of uncovering something crucial, but the risk of being discovered was ever-present.

As the operatives continued their preparations, Ethan, Hale, Cline, and Drake remained hidden, their hearts pounding with the weight of the moment. The stakes were higher than ever, and the danger was more immediate. Every decision they made from this point forward could determine their fate and the success or failure of their mission.

In the dim light of the warehouse, with the unseen enemy closing in, the suspense and tension were almost unbearable. The outcome of their perilous journey was hanging by a thread, and the shadows of the Black Veil loomed ever closer.

7

The Threshold of Deception

The chill of night had fully descended by the time Ethan, Hale, Cline, and Drake crept through the darkened streets toward the warehouse where the Black Veil was rumored to be finalizing their plans. The once-familiar cityscape now felt like a labyrinth of dangers, each turn and shadow brimming with potential threats. The urgency in their mission made every step more perilous.

Ethan's pulse thrummed in his ears as he glanced at Hale, who led them with a steady hand. The warehouse loomed ahead, its dark silhouette outlined against the sparse city lights. The group moved in silence, their breaths visible in the cold night air, the weight of their objective heavy on their shoulders.

They reached a point of concealment just outside the warehouse's perimeter, hidden behind a rusting stack of shipping containers. Hale peered through binoculars, scrutinizing the activity inside. The faint glow of lights from within revealed the silhouettes of several figures—some moving briskly, others engaged in animated conversation. The tension in the air was palpable, and every sense was on high alert.

"We need to get closer," Hale whispered, lowering the binoculars. "But we must avoid detection."

Cline nodded, her eyes scanning the area for any signs of security or patrols. "Let's find an entry point. If we can get inside and gather more information, we might be able to figure out their next move."

They carefully approached the warehouse, their movements deliberate and cautious. Ethan's nerves were on edge as they neared a side entrance—a metal door slightly ajar, its hinges rusty and unsteady. Hale inspected the door, noting its condition.

"This looks like our best chance," Hale said. "We'll slip inside through here. Stay alert and move quietly."

The door creaked open, and they slipped into the warehouse's shadowed interior. The scent of dust and rust filled their nostrils, and the noise of machinery and voices was louder now, reverberating through the vast space. They moved cautiously, hugging the walls and using the clutter of old crates and machinery as cover.

As they advanced deeper into the warehouse, Ethan noticed a dim light filtering through a small window high up on one wall. The sounds of conversation grew clearer, punctuated by occasional bursts of laughter and clinking metal. The atmosphere was tense but animated, suggesting a critical meeting or planning session was underway.

They found a vantage point near a stack of crates, allowing them to observe the central area of the warehouse. From their position, they could see a large table surrounded by operatives in Black Veil gear. Maps, blueprints, and various electronic devices were spread across the table, and a projector displayed a detailed layout of what appeared to be a high-security facility.

Ethan's gaze was drawn to a figure at the head of the table—a tall man with an authoritative presence, his face obscured by a mask. The Black Veil operatives seemed to defer to him, their discussions and movements coordinated with a sense of purpose and urgency.

Drake's voice was barely a whisper as he leaned closer. "That's Viktor Draven. He's the head of the Black Veil's operations. If anyone knows what their plan is, it's him."

Ethan felt a surge of apprehension. Viktor Draven was notorious for his cunning and ruthlessness. The thought of being so close to him was unsettling, but they needed to gather information to stop the Black Veil's plans.

The group watched as Draven addressed his operatives, his voice low but commanding. "Our window of opportunity is closing. We have a limited time to execute our plan. The target must be in our possession before the authorities catch wind of our activities."

The words sent a chill through Ethan. The "target" could only refer to Hale's research—the key to the Black Veil's plan. They needed to act quickly to thwart whatever scheme Draven had in mind.

As the discussion continued, Ethan noticed a side door leading to a smaller office off to one side. It was partially open, and a faint light glowed from within. "There might be more information in that office," Ethan whispered to Hale. "If we can access it, we might find something crucial."

Hale nodded, his eyes scanning the area for any signs of patrols. "Alright, let's move quickly but carefully."

The group stealthily made their way toward the office, avoiding the main area where the operatives were focused on their briefing. The door creaked as they entered, and they slipped inside, closing it behind them.

The office was cluttered with old filing cabinets and stacks of documents. Ethan's eyes were drawn to a desk in the corner, where several files and a laptop lay open. He approached the desk and began sifting through the papers, his heart racing as he searched for anything that might reveal the Black Veil's plans.

Cline worked on the laptop, her fingers flying over the keyboard as she accessed files and emails. "I'm searching for any clues about their timeline or specific targets," she said, her voice tense.

Drake, still visibly anxious, kept watch at the door, his eyes darting nervously. "We need to hurry. If we're discovered, it's over."

As Ethan and Cline worked feverishly, a sudden noise from the main area of the warehouse made them freeze. The unmistakable sound of footsteps and voices approaching sent a jolt of fear through them. They exchanged worried glances, knowing that their time was running out.

Cline's eyes widened as she read a file on the laptop. "This is it. They're planning to execute their operation within the next 24 hours. The target is to be secured and extracted before dawn tomorrow."

The urgency of the situation was undeniable. Ethan felt a surge of determination. They had to get this information to Hale and find a way to stop the Black Veil before it was too late.

Just then, the door to the office creaked open, and the shadow of a figure fell across the floor. Ethan's breath caught in his throat as he saw a Black Veil operative standing in the doorway, his eyes scanning the room.

Without thinking, Ethan grabbed a nearby chair and hurled it at the operative, causing him to stumble backward. Cline quickly shut down the laptop and grabbed the files, while Hale and Drake moved to defend their position.

The warehouse erupted into chaos as alarms began to blare, the sound echoing through the vast space. The operatives in the main area reacted with swift precision, converging on the office.

Ethan, Hale, Cline, and Drake raced toward the back exit, their hearts pounding with the adrenaline of their escape. The warehouse was alive with noise and movement, the once-clear path now a frantic scramble for safety.

They burst through the side door and into the night, their breaths coming in ragged gasps as they sprinted through the streets. The Black Veil was now fully aware of their presence, and the chase was on.

As they reached the safety of an alleyway, Ethan glanced back at the warehouse, its lights now a distant beacon in the darkness. They had narrowly escaped, but the threat was far from over. The Black Veil's plans were set in motion, and the clock was ticking.

In the darkness of the alley, with the echoes of their pursuit fading, Ethan knew that their battle against the Black Veil had reached a critical juncture. The stakes were higher than ever, and the path ahead was fraught with danger and uncertainty. The threshold of deception had been crossed, and their mission to thwart the Black Veil's plans had become a race against time.

8

The Phantom's Gambit

Ethan's lungs burned as he and the others fled through the labyrinth of alleys, their escape from the warehouse a narrow victory that had left them breathless and on edge. The night air was cool but felt heavy with the tension of their pursuit. The Black Veil was no longer just a looming threat; it was a palpable danger, and their escape had only heightened their sense of vulnerability.

The group made their way to an old, abandoned office building that Hale had suggested as a temporary safe house. Its grim façade and boarded-up windows made it an unlikely target for surveillance, but they needed to regroup and plan their next move. Inside, the space was dimly lit by a few flickering lights, the silence of the building a stark contrast to the chaos they had just escaped.

Hale quickly set up a perimeter and checked for any signs of tampering. "We need to assess our situation," he said, his voice steady despite the strain. "We've got intel on their operation, but we don't have a clear picture yet. We need to figure out their exact plan and how we can disrupt it."

Ethan nodded, his mind racing as he tried to piece together the fragments of information they had gathered. "We know they're moving within the next 24 hours, and their target is crucial. If we don't act fast, they'll have what they need, and we'll be left with nothing."

Cline, still catching her breath, began sorting through the documents they had retrieved. "The data points to a high-security facility, but it doesn't specify the exact location. We need to cross-reference this with what we know about the Black Veil's operations."

Drake, his face pale and drawn, slumped into a chair. "I've never seen them this organized. They must have someone inside who's feeding them information."

Ethan glanced at him, his expression serious. "We need to assume they're always one step ahead. We have to be smarter and more unpredictable. If they're anticipating our moves, we need to create confusion."

As they worked, the sound of footsteps echoed through the empty building. Each noise made Ethan's heart race, but Hale's sharp eyes quickly identified the source—an old security system that had been triggered by their entry. The beeping of a malfunctioning alarm was a small but constant reminder of their precarious situation.

They continued their preparations, going over every detail of the documents. Hale laid out a map of the city and began plotting potential locations for the Black Veil's target. "They're likely using a location that's secure and secluded, somewhere they can operate without attracting too much attention."

Cline looked over the map, her eyes narrowing as she traced potential locations with her finger. "What if they're using a decoy? They might have set up false leads to throw us off."

Hale's expression was grim. "It's possible. They're known for their deception and misdirection. We need to account for that in our planning."

The building's silence was shattered by a sudden, loud crash—a sound of something heavy falling or breaking. Ethan's heart jumped into his throat. The sense of being hunted was ever-present, and every unexpected noise heightened their paranoia.

Hale and Ethan moved cautiously towards the source of the noise, their steps echoing eerily through the empty hallways. They found a broken window and a scattering of debris—a sign that someone or something had been here recently.

"It looks like we're not alone," Hale said, his voice tense. "We need to be extra cautious. The Black Veil might have found us."

The group returned to their temporary base, their nerves on edge. Ethan could feel the weight of their situation pressing down on him. The Black Veil was not just a faceless enemy; they were an organized, ruthless force that had managed to stay several steps ahead.

Cline's phone buzzed, and she answered quickly, her voice low and urgent. "What do you have?" She listened for a moment, her expression shifting from concern to surprise. "We need to verify this. Thanks for the tip."

She hung up and turned to the group, her face reflecting a mixture of hope and anxiety. "That was a contact from my network. They've identified a possible location—a warehouse on the outskirts of the city. It fits the profile for a high-security facility."

Hale's eyes narrowed as he considered the information. "It's a lead, but we need to be careful. If it's a trap, it could be a setup to lure us in."

Ethan nodded, the sense of urgency mounting. "We don't have much time. We need to check it out, but we have to stay vigilant."

They prepared to move out, their senses heightened and their movements swift. The abandoned office building's grim atmosphere seemed to weigh heavily on them as they left, the echoes of their departure lingering in the silent space.

As they approached the new warehouse, the sense of foreboding grew. The building was isolated, surrounded by high fences and guarded by security cameras. The perimeter was well-protected, a clear indication of the importance of whatever was inside.

Hale led them through a series of back alleys and hidden routes, using his knowledge of the area to navigate towards a less conspicuous approach. They found a vantage point overlooking the warehouse and observed the activity below.

The scene was bustling with activity. Operatives in Black Veil gear were moving about, carrying crates and equipment. The intensity of their actions suggested a major operation was underway.

Ethan's pulse quickened as he observed the scene. "We need to get closer, but we have to be careful not to get caught."

The group moved cautiously, finding a spot to conceal themselves near a side entrance. Hale inspected the area and found a small, barely noticeable door that led into the building. They prepared to enter, their breaths shallow with anticipation.

Just as they were about to make their move, a sudden flash of light and the sound of approaching vehicles made them freeze. Black Veil operatives were arriving in trucks, their presence signaling an escalation in the operation.

Ethan's heart raced as they took cover, the gravity of the situation sinking in. The Black Veil was clearly preparing for something significant, and the risk of being discovered was high. They had to gather as much information as possible and find a way to disrupt the Black Veil's plans.

As the operatives continued their activities, Ethan, Hale, Cline, and Drake remained hidden, their senses on high alert. The warehouse was now a hive of activity, and the stakes had never been higher. The Phantom's Gambit was in full play, and their survival depended on their ability to stay ahead of an enemy that was always lurking in the shadows.

9

The Echo of Betrayal

The night's chill seemed to seep into Ethan's bones as he, Hale, Cline, and Drake waited in the shadow of the warehouse, their breaths forming misty clouds in the cold air. The Black Veil's operations had intensified, with trucks and armed guards now forming a tight perimeter around the building. Every sense was on high alert as they prepared for their most dangerous incursion yet.

Ethan glanced at his watch, noting the passing minutes. The urgency of their mission pressed heavily on him. With every moment that ticked by, the likelihood of discovering the Black Veil's true intentions—or being discovered themselves—grew.

Hale surveyed the perimeter through binoculars, his brow furrowed. "The security is tighter than expected. They must be preparing for something significant."

Cline, crouched beside a stack of crates, checked the handheld scanner she had been using to detect any electronic surveillance or traps. "We've got an array of sensors and cameras to bypass. This won't be easy."

Drake, visibly tense, whispered, "We're running out of time. We need to get inside and find out what they're planning. The last thing we need is to be caught in the middle of their operation."

Hale nodded, then pointed to a side entrance with a security panel. "That's our best bet. If we can hack into the system and disable the alarms, we might have a chance."

They moved swiftly but cautiously toward the entrance, Ethan's pulse racing with each step. The night was unnervingly quiet, the only sounds their muffled movements and the distant hum of machinery inside the warehouse.

As they approached the entrance, Hale pulled out a set of tools and began working on the security panel. His fingers moved deftly, bypassing the lock and wiring with practiced precision. The display flickered, then went dark, indicating that they had successfully disabled the system.

"We're in," Hale whispered, opening the door just enough to slip through.

The group entered the dimly lit corridor, the air heavy with the smell of metal and oil. They moved quickly through the narrow passage, their steps echoing softly. Every shadow seemed to hide a potential threat, and Ethan's instincts were on high alert.

They emerged into a larger room filled with crates and industrial equipment. From here, they could hear the murmur of voices and the clinking of metal—a stark reminder of the Black Veil's ongoing activities. Ethan signaled for silence as they advanced, sticking to the shadows and using the crates for cover.

Cline approached a small control panel mounted on the wall and began interfacing with it, trying to gather information on the warehouse's layout and any active security systems. "If we can access their internal network, we might find details on their plans," she said, her voice low and focused.

Suddenly, a loud crash echoed through the warehouse, followed by the distinct sound of shouting. Ethan's heart skipped a beat as he glanced toward the source of the commotion. It seemed that the Black Veil operatives were on high alert, their movements becoming more frantic.

"Something's wrong," Hale murmured, his eyes darting around. "They're definitely preparing for something big."

Drake's face grew pale. "I think we might have been set up. This could be a diversion."

Before Ethan could respond, a series of footsteps approached from the corridor they had just entered. The sound was unmistakable—Black Veil operatives coming their way. Ethan's adrenaline surged as he signaled for the group to hide behind a stack of crates.

They huddled together, holding their breaths as the operatives passed by, their voices discussing the recent security breach. The tension was palpable, each second stretching into an eternity. Ethan could see the operatives' faces through the gaps in the crates, their expressions tense and determined.

Once the operatives had moved out of sight, Hale carefully peered around the crates. "We need to find another way to gather information. If they're on to us, we need to be cautious."

Cline looked up from her control panel, her face pale. "I've accessed some files, but they're encrypted. It's going to take time to decrypt them, and we don't have much of that."

Drake's anxiety was evident. "If we're being set up, we need to get out before they lock down the facility."

Hale nodded in agreement. "We'll have to act quickly. We need to find a way to access the main control room or server room. That's where we'll get the most crucial information."

As they moved toward the main area of the warehouse, Ethan noticed a familiar face among the Black Veil operatives—a man who had previously worked with them, someone Ethan had trusted. The sight was a gut-wrenching realization: a betrayal from within.

"Is that—" Ethan began, his voice choked with disbelief.

Hale glanced in the direction Ethan was pointing and his eyes widened in recognition. "It is. That's Marcus Reynolds. He was supposed to be one of us."

The betrayal stung deep, the realization that someone within their ranks had aligned with the Black Veil was a harsh blow. Ethan's resolve hardened. They had to press on, not just for their mission but for justice.

They approached a locked door leading to what appeared to be the central control room. Hale got to work on the lock, his fingers working with a frantic urgency. "If Reynolds is involved, this operation is even more dangerous than we thought."

The lock clicked open, and they slipped into the control room, which was filled with monitors and complex equipment. Cline immediately went to work, her fingers flying over the keyboard as she accessed the system.

Ethan scanned the room, his eyes landing on a set of schematics and plans pinned to a wall. He moved closer, his pulse racing as he examined the documents. They detailed a high-profile heist planned for the following day—a sophisticated operation that aimed to infiltrate a secure facility and steal critical data.

"This is it," Ethan said, his voice grim. "They're targeting a major government database. If they succeed, it could cripple national security."

Cline's eyes widened as she decrypted a file on the computer. "The plans are detailed. They've even identified escape routes and contingencies. This is a well-orchestrated operation."

As they gathered the information, Ethan heard the distant sound of approaching vehicles and the hum of engines. The Black Veil's operation was clearly in full swing, and they were running out of time.

"We need to get out of here," Hale said urgently. "If they're mobilizing, we'll be caught in the crossfire."

They made their way back toward the entrance, their hearts pounding with the weight of their mission. The warehouse was now a hive of activity, the Black Veil's plans coming to fruition. They had uncovered crucial information, but the sense of betrayal and the looming threat made their task even more urgent.

As they exited the warehouse and disappeared into the night, Ethan felt the burden of their mission heavier than ever. The Echo of Betrayal had reverberated through their ranks, and their fight against the Black Veil had become a battle against not just an enemy, but the shadows within their own organization.

10

The Fractured Alliance

Dawn was still hours away when Ethan, Hale, Cline, and Drake convened in the secluded, dimly lit basement of an old library. The room was cluttered with old books and musty furniture, its very air thick with dust and the weight of secrets. The day's mission had pushed them to their limits, and the information they had retrieved from the warehouse was both a beacon and a burden. They had exposed the Black Veil's plan, but the realization of their betrayal had left a crack in their foundation.

Hale paced back and forth, his normally steady demeanor showing signs of strain. "We've got the details of their operation, but the complexity is staggering. We need to alert authorities, but the infiltration is too deep. They've anticipated our every move."

Ethan leaned against a table covered in blueprints and documents, his face etched with fatigue. "We need to strategize. If Reynolds was compromised, we have to assume there are others. We can't trust anyone outside this room."

Drake, still shaken, looked up from a stack of files. "What if the Black Veil has other plans? If they can corrupt our own people, they might have set up contingencies to throw us off completely."

Cline's fingers danced over a laptop, her eyes scanning rapidly. "I'm working on decrypting the rest of the files. There's a lot more here, and we need to understand every detail if we're going to counteract their plans."

The tension in the room was palpable, the silence broken only by the occasional rustle of paper or the clatter of a keyboard. The weight of their situation pressed heavily on each member of the team. The Black Veil's operation was imminent, and their next move needed to be precise and timely.

A sudden, loud crash echoed from above, followed by hurried footsteps. Ethan's heart skipped a beat as he signaled for the others to remain silent. The basement's only exit was the narrow stairwell leading up to the library's main floor—a potential bottleneck if they were to be discovered.

The footsteps grew louder, and the sound of a door being forced open sent a shiver down Ethan's spine. He motioned for everyone to take cover behind the large wooden bookshelves. They crouched in the darkness, their breaths shallow and their senses heightened.

Through the thin walls, Ethan could hear voices and the clattering of metal. His mind raced with possibilities. Were they being raided, or was this an attempt by the Black Veil to flush them out?

Cline, her face pale under the dim light, whispered urgently, "We need to find out who's upstairs. If it's Black Veil operatives, we're in serious trouble."

Hale nodded, his face grim. "I'll check it out. Stay here and be ready to move if necessary."

With a swift, silent movement, Hale crept up the stairs, his footsteps barely audible. Ethan, Cline, and Drake waited in tense silence, their ears straining to catch any sound from above.

Minutes felt like hours as they waited, each creak of the old building making their nerves fray. Finally, Hale's figure reappeared at the top of the stairs, his expression a mix of relief and alarm.

"It's not Black Veil," Hale reported in a low voice. "It's a group of local thieves. They're scavenging for valuables."

Drake let out a sigh of relief. "For a moment, I thought we were compromised."

Hale nodded, his eyes narrowing. "We might still be. Their presence means we're not the only ones with an interest in this place. We need to be extra cautious."

Cline had managed to decrypt more files by now. "I've got some information on their next target—an underground facility where they're planning to execute their heist. We need to get there before they do."

Ethan nodded, his expression resolute. "We'll head out immediately. We need to find a way to disrupt their operation and minimize the damage."

They packed up their things and prepared to leave, their minds focused on the impending mission. The knowledge of a traitor in their midst made every decision fraught with uncertainty. They knew they couldn't trust anyone outside their immediate group, and the fear of further betrayal loomed large.

As they exited the library, the early morning air was cool and crisp. The city was just beginning to wake, but their time was running short. They had to reach the underground facility and neutralize the Black Veil's plans before it was too late.

They made their way through the city, their movements quick and deliberate.

Hale's local knowledge guided them through back alleys and lesser-known routes, avoiding the main roads where they might attract attention. The fear of being followed was ever-present, and they kept their eyes and ears open for any signs of pursuit.

Arriving at the underground facility, they found it heavily guarded and fortified. The sheer scale of the operation was intimidating, with guards stationed at various points and surveillance cameras covering every angle.

Ethan and the team took cover behind a stack of crates, their breaths coming in short, nervous bursts. The Black Veil operatives were busy preparing their equipment and discussing their plans. Ethan could see the tension in their movements, a reflection of their own anxious anticipation.

Hale pulled out a small device that emitted a signal jammer. "This will help us disable their communications temporarily. We'll use the confusion to get inside."

With the jammer activated, the facility's security systems began to falter. The cameras flickered and the guards' radios went silent. It was their opportunity to move.

Cline led the way, her expertise guiding them through the maze of corridors and security checkpoints. They navigated the facility with a blend of stealth and urgency, their senses on high alert for any signs of detection.

As they approached the central control room, the tension was almost unbearable. The stakes had never been higher, and the sense of imminent danger was palpable. They knew that any misstep could lead to their capture or worse.

They reached the control room, and Cline immediately set to work on the terminal, her fingers moving rapidly over the keyboard. "I'm accessing their mainframe now. We need to stop their operation and secure the facility."

The door to the control room burst open with a loud clang. The group froze as several Black Veil operatives stormed in, their weapons drawn. The element of surprise had been lost, and the battle for control of the facility was now underway.

Ethan, Hale, Cline, and Drake fought fiercely, their movements a blur of adrenaline and determination. They managed to hold their ground, but the odds were against them. The Black Veil operatives were well-trained and ruthless.

As the fight raged on, Ethan's mind raced with strategies and contingencies. The realization that their mission might fail—and that the consequences of such a failure were dire—pressed heavily upon him.

In the midst of the chaos, Cline's voice cut through the noise. "I've almost got it! Just a little longer!"

With a final, desperate push, Ethan and his team fought their way through the remaining operatives. The control room was now a battleground, but their determination and resilience shone through.

Cline managed to complete the final sequence on the terminal, halting the Black Veil's plans. The facility's alarms blared, signaling a lockdown.

As the dust began to settle, Ethan and his team stood victorious but exhausted. The Fractured Alliance had weathered yet another storm, but the cracks in their unity and the looming threat of the Black Veil remained.

The facility was secure, but the fight was far from over. With the Black Veil's plans thwarted, they knew that the true challenge lay ahead in uncovering the full extent of the betrayal and ensuring that their mission would ultimately succeed.

11

The Collapse

Ethan and his team emerged from the underground facility, their faces grim and their bodies bruised from the fierce battle. The early morning light, now a promising hue of orange and pink, contrasted sharply with the darkness of the facility they had just escaped. They had succeeded in halting the Black Veil's operation, but the victory felt hollow in the wake of the betrayals and constant threats they faced.

The group gathered in a secluded alleyway, a safe distance from the facility. Ethan's mind raced as he reviewed their next steps, but fatigue and the weight of their mission made it hard to focus. Hale, still catching his breath, glanced around nervously. "We need to regroup and reassess. The Black Veil's plans are disrupted, but they're not done. They'll come after us, and we need to be ready."

Drake, his eyes darkened with exhaustion, nodded in agreement. "We've taken out one operation, but they're a vast organization. We need to find out what their next move is."

Cline, her face pale from the exertion and stress, was reviewing the data she had managed to secure from the facility. "I'm going through the files we retrieved. There's a lot of information, but it's crucial to find any leads on their upcoming activities."

As Cline worked, Ethan's phone buzzed with an incoming message. He glanced at the screen and his heart sank. It was from an unknown number, but the message was clear: "You've meddled with our plans. Now you'll pay the price."

The message was a threat, and the chilling implication was that the Black Veil was closing in on them. Ethan's jaw tightened with resolve. "We've been compromised. We need to find a secure location and figure out our next move."

The group moved quickly through the city streets, their nerves frayed and their senses heightened. Every shadow and passing vehicle seemed like a potential threat. They eventually found refuge in an abandoned warehouse on the outskirts of town. The building was dilapidated and empty, its walls covered in graffiti and its floors strewn with debris. It was far from ideal, but it offered some measure of security.

Inside, they took stock of their situation. Hale set up a perimeter with a makeshift barricade, while Cline continued to sift through the files on her laptop. Ethan and Drake checked the building's entry points and ensured they had a plan in place if they needed to make a quick escape.

Hours passed in tense silence, the only sounds the occasional clatter of metal or the rustle of papers. Ethan felt a gnawing sense of dread as he considered the threat they had received. The Black Veil was ruthless, and their warning was a clear sign that they were prepared to retaliate.

Cline finally looked up from her laptop, her face pale but determined. "I've found something. There's a reference to a secure meeting place—a hidden facility where high-level operations are discussed. If we can find it, we might uncover the next phase of their plans."

Ethan's heart raced. "Where is it?"

Cline hesitated for a moment, then handed Ethan a printed map. "The coordinates point to a location on the outskirts of the city. It's heavily guarded, but it's our best lead."

Drake's eyes narrowed with concern. "It's a risk, but it's our only option. We need to find out what the Black Veil is planning next."

As they prepared to leave, Ethan's phone buzzed again. This time, it was a call from a blocked number. His pulse quickened as he answered, "Ethan."

A distorted voice on the other end replied, "You've been a thorn in our side, Ethan. The next phase of our plan is already in motion. If you think you can stop us, you're mistaken."

Before Ethan could respond, the call ended abruptly. The threat was unmistakable, and the urgency of their mission intensified.

The team left the warehouse and made their way to the coordinates on the map. The city's streets were eerily quiet as they approached the hidden facility, their nerves stretched taut. They navigated through a maze of alleys and back roads, their senses on high alert.

The hidden facility was a stark contrast to the abandoned warehouse. It was a modern, high-tech building with a sleek exterior and state-of-the-art security. The presence of armed guards and surveillance cameras made it clear that they were about to enter a high-stakes environment.

Hale and Cline used their skills to disable the security systems and gain access to the building. The infiltration was tense and precarious, but they managed to slip inside without being detected.

The interior of the facility was a maze of corridors and high-tech equipment. They moved cautiously, their footsteps silent on the polished floors. Ethan could feel the weight of their mission pressing down on him, the knowledge that they were in enemy territory heightening their vulnerability.

They reached a control room filled with monitors and computers. Cline immediately began accessing the system, her fingers flying over the keyboard as she searched for valuable information.

As Cline worked, Ethan scanned the room, his eyes darting from one monitor to another. The facility was filled with data on various Black Veil operations and projects, but their immediate concern was finding the details on the next phase of the plan.

Suddenly, the facility's alarms blared, their shrill sound cutting through the silence. Ethan's heart raced as he realized that their presence had been detected. The Black Veil was onto them.

"Move!" Ethan shouted, grabbing Cline and leading the group toward an exit. The facility was now in lockdown mode, with security personnel and automated defenses activated. The challenge of escaping became exponentially more difficult.

They fought their way through the facility, their movements a chaotic blend of desperation and determination. Ethan could see the Black Veil operatives closing in, their faces set with grim determination.

As they neared an exit, the building's security system engaged a series of automated defenses. Doors slammed shut, and a barrage of automated turrets sprang to life, targeting anything that moved. The team was trapped, their path to freedom blocked by a maze of obstacles.

In the midst of the chaos, Cline's voice cut through the noise. "I've almost hacked into the system! Just hold on!"

Ethan and the team fought off the operatives and navigated the automated defenses with a combination of strategy and brute force. The fight was relentless, and the stakes had never been higher.

Finally, Cline managed to disable the security systems, and the automated defenses powered down. They took their chance and fled the facility, their hearts pounding with the rush of adrenaline and relief.

As they emerged into the night, the city's skyline stretched before them, the promise of safety a distant hope. The Collapse of their operation had been a narrow escape, and the full extent of the Black Veil's plans remained unclear.

They regrouped in a safe house, their faces etched with exhaustion and determination. The threat of the Black Veil was far from over, but they had managed to survive another day. The battle was ongoing, and the challenge ahead was greater than ever.

Ethan looked around at his team, their resolve unwavering despite the setbacks. The fight against the Black Veil had become a battle not just for survival, but for the future of their world. And as the dawn approached, they knew that the real test of their strength and unity was yet to come.

12

The Final Gambit

The city lay shrouded in an unsettling silence, its usual hustle and bustle replaced by an eerie calm. Ethan, Hale, Cline, and Drake gathered in the dimly lit, cramped confines of a hidden bunker located deep beneath a derelict building. The walls were lined with old maps, blueprints, and scattered equipment, remnants of their arduous journey. The weight of their mission pressed heavily upon them, as their recent escape from the Black Veil's facility had only heightened the urgency of their situation.

Ethan stared at the cluttered table, which was now covered with the information they had managed to gather. The recent series of events had taken their toll, leaving him feeling both physically and mentally drained. Yet, there was no time to rest. The Black Veil's next move was imminent, and the stakes had never been higher.

Cline, her face illuminated by the flickering light of a laptop screen, was deep in concentration. "I've managed to piece together most of their plans," she said, her voice tight with frustration. "They're targeting a major infrastructure hub—one that's crucial to the city's power grid. If they succeed, it could plunge the entire city into darkness, chaos, and give them the perfect cover for their operations."

Drake, still nursing wounds from their last confrontation, clenched his jaw. "We need to stop them before they reach the hub. We've lost too much already."

Hale, who had been pacing the room with a sense of urgency, nodded in agreement. "We need a plan, and it needs to be executed flawlessly. The Black Veil will have anticipated any conventional approaches."

Ethan's mind raced as he considered their options. The facility they had just escaped from had revealed the breadth of the Black Veil's influence, but they were no closer to understanding their full strategy. The hub was a critical target, and the idea of it being compromised filled him with dread.

"We need to intercept them before they get close to the hub," Ethan said, determination lacing his voice. "But we also need to figure out how to neutralize their operatives and their security measures."

The team sprang into action, their movements coordinated and efficient. Hale and Drake worked on preparing their equipment, while Cline continued to analyze the data. The tension in the room was palpable, the knowledge that their next move could either save the city or lead to catastrophic failure weighing heavily on them.

As they made their way to the outskirts of the city where the infrastructure hub was located, the night air was filled with an oppressive sense of foreboding. They moved stealthily through the shadows, their senses alert to every sound and movement. The hub loomed ahead, its darkened silhouette a stark reminder of the challenge they faced.

The perimeter of the hub was heavily guarded, with multiple layers of security and surveillance systems in place. Ethan and his team took up their positions, their breaths shallow as they assessed the situation. The Black Veil's operatives were already in motion, their movements calculated and precise.

"We need to disable their security systems first," Cline whispered, her eyes scanning the hub's defenses. "Once that's done, we can move in and stop them."

With a deep breath, the team set to work. Hale and Drake approached the security systems, their expertise allowing them to bypass the initial layers of protection. Cline worked on hacking into the control systems, her fingers flying over the keyboard as she navigated the complex network of security protocols.

As they worked, Ethan kept a vigilant watch. The night seemed to stretch endlessly, each passing minute amplifying the tension. He could see the Black Veil operatives moving closer to their objective, their faces concealed by masks and their intentions shrouded in secrecy.

A sudden burst of static from Ethan's radio interrupted the silence. "Ethan, we've got a problem," Cline's voice crackled through. "The Black Veil has deployed additional security. We're running out of time."

Ethan's heart raced as he saw the additional guards arriving, their numbers and equipment making their task even more daunting. "We need to accelerate our plan. Cline, how long until you're done?"

"I'm almost there," Cline replied, her voice strained with concentration. "But we need to act now."

Ethan signaled to Hale and Drake, who prepared for the next phase of their operation. The team moved with a sense of urgency, their actions synchronized as they prepared to breach the hub's defenses.

As they made their way through the security systems, the tension reached a fever pitch. Every step felt like a gamble, each move a potential risk. The hub was now a hive of activity, with the Black Veil's operatives making their final preparations for the attack.

With a final keystroke, Cline disabled the security systems, allowing the team to slip through the defenses. They navigated the complex labyrinth of the hub, their movements swift and deliberate. The stakes were higher than ever, and failure was not an option.

They reached the control room, where the Black Veil's operatives were busy preparing their equipment. The room was filled with the hum of machinery and the flickering glow of monitors. Ethan and his team prepared for the confrontation, their hearts pounding with a mixture of fear and determination.

The ensuing battle was fierce and chaotic. The Black Veil operatives were well-trained and relentless, their determination matching Ethan's team's resolve. The clash of weapons and the sound of shattering glass filled the room as both sides fought for control.

In the midst of the conflict, Ethan caught sight of the Black Veil's leader—a figure whose face remained obscured by a mask. The leader's presence was imposing, and Ethan could sense the weight of their sinister plans.

With a final, desperate effort, Ethan and his team pushed through the chaos. They fought their way to the central control panel, where Cline worked furiously to disable the Black Veil's equipment. The struggle was intense, and the outcome hung in the balance.

As the battle reached its climax, Ethan managed to confront the Black Veil's leader. Their confrontation was a whirlwind of emotion and determination, each move and counter-move driven by the knowledge that the fate of the city rested on their shoulders.

With a final surge of effort, Ethan and his team overcame the Black Veil's operatives. The control panel was secured, and the imminent threat was neutralized. The hub's systems powered down, and the city was spared from disaster.

Exhausted but victorious, Ethan and his team regrouped in the aftermath of the battle. The hub was now secure, and the Black Veil's plans had been thwarted. But the victory came at a cost, and the scars of their struggle were evident in their faces and their spirits.

As dawn broke over the city, Ethan and his team stood amidst the ruins of their confrontation, their hearts heavy with the knowledge that the fight was far from over. The Black Veil's reach was extensive, and their true intentions remained a mystery.

But for now, the immediate threat had been vanquished. The city was safe, and the team had proven their resilience and determination. As they prepared to leave the hub, their minds were already focused on the challenges that lay ahead.

The Final Gambit had been a decisive moment in their struggle, but it was only the beginning of a larger battle. Ethan knew that the road ahead would be fraught with danger and uncertainty, but he was ready to face it with his team by his side. The fight against the Black Veil was far from over, and their quest for justice and truth would continue.